WILTSHIRE
IN PHOTOGRAPHS

DIANE VOSE

AMBERLEY

First published 2022

Amberley Publishing
The Hill, Stroud
Gloucestershire, GL5 4EP

www.amberley-books.com

Copyright © Diane Vose, 2022

The right of Diane Vose to be identified as the Author of this work has been
asserted in accordance with the Copyrights, Designs and Patents Act 1988.

ISBN 978 1 4456 9493 1 (print)
ISBN 978 1 4456 9494 8 (ebook)

British Library Cataloguing in Publication Data.
A catalogue record for this book is available from the British Library.

Typesetting by SJmagic DESIGN SERVICES, India.
Printed in the UK.

ACKNOWLEDGEMENTS

I would like to thank my wonderful parents, Christine and William Vose; sister, Carole Varga; and grandparents, Ken and Helen Forsythe, for their support and encouragement over the years with my interest and love of photography. It was my dad who supplied the money to purchase my first camera – the 110 – at aged seven, which was then put to good use in taking pictures of friends, family and landscapes. I would also like to thank former sub-editor Jo Bayne, who I worked with for many years on the *Wiltshire Gazette* and *Herald*, for helping me write the introduction to this book.

Thanks to everyone at Bowood House and Gardens for allowing me to photograph the changing seasons at this beautiful Wiltshire landmark. Thank you to Help for Heroes, who allowed me to photograph their home base at Tedworth House in Tidworth. I would also like to thank the Facebook group 'Beautiful Wiltshire', who inspired me to visit so many wonderful locations for the book. Thanks to Angeline Wilcox at Amberley Publishing, who saw my images and approached me about doing this book on Wiltshire. Thank you also to Jenny Stephens for her help throughout the process.

ABOUT THE PHOTOGRAPHER

Diane Vose is a photographer based in the county of Wiltshire. On moving to the county fifteen years ago she fell in love with Wiltshire's big skies, rolling countryside and historic past. She loves to be outdoors whatever the weather and enjoys walking in the rural landscape, capturing its timeless beauty on camera. Being a former press photographer who travelled extensively while on photographic assignments, Diane was as much captivated by the Wiltshire towns and villages she encountered as she was by the magical landscape she travelled through.

Diane has used Nikon photographic equipment for the past twenty years. Starting with Nikon's first digital camera, the D1, right through to her current camera, D4s, which is combined with 17–35 mm and 70–200 mm lenses. Her former life as a press photographer needed outstanding camera equipment, an eye for a good picture and a great deal of patience, which rather lends itself to her new vocation as a landscape and outdoor photographer.

Twitter: @VoseDiane
Instagram: @vosediane

INTRODUCTION

The beautiful county of Wiltshire boasts two World Heritage sites: Stonehenge and Avebury. These two magnificent Neolithic monuments have fascinated people for thousands of years and continue to draw millions of visitors from across the United Kingdom and around the world. There are a large number of other Neolithic sites in the county, including Silbury Hill, the largest Neolithic mound in Europe, and nearby West Kennet Long Barrow, a large Neolithic chambered tomb.

The Romans and Anglo-Saxons also left their mark upon the landscape with hill forts at Cleyhill, Bratton Camp and 'Ethundun', located in the village of Edington, where King Alfred defeated the Danes in 878 and changed the course of history across the United Kingdom.

Wiltshire is also known for its beautiful landscape. Almost half of the county is designated an Area of Outstanding Natural Beauty. Salisbury Plain covers 300 square miles and is famous for its archaeology. The plain is now used mainly for military training and is closed to the public, which makes it an impressive wildlife haven. The chalk downland landscape supports thirteen types of rare plants and sixty-seven rare invertebrates. Imber, the lost village on the plain, was commandeered by the Ministry of Defence in 1943 as a wartime military training ground – the villagers were evicted from their homes, never to return. The village is open to the public at Christmas every year. The white horses of Wiltshire have become a symbol for the county. There are eight of them, at Westbury, Cherhill, Devizes, Alton Barnes, Pewsey, Hackpen and Broad Town.

Wiltshire also offers the visitor charming villages with chocolate-box views of thatched cottages and parish churches. The villages of Lacock and Castle Combe have been chosen as locations for many films and television period dramas and visitors will probably recognise the gold stone cottages, pretty bridges and streams or quaint high streets. The towns throughout Wiltshire offer independent shopping, weekly markets and history on the doorstep with old buildings, museums and other attractions.

I hope *Wiltshire in Photographs* will give the reader a visual tour of the county, showcasing its ancient past, beautiful countryside and pretty villages and towns. It's a county where the past and the present work together in perfect harmony.

ANCIENT WILTSHIRE

Avebury Neolithic henge at sunrise

Piggledene field of sarsen stones

Silbury Hill prehistoric mound surrounded by water

Lockeridge Dene sarsen
stones in the village of
Lockeridge

Knap Hill, Neolithic causewayed enclosure in the Pewsey Vale

Adam's Grave, Neolithic long barrow, Pewsey Vale

Martinsell Hill's Iron
Age hill fort, near
Milton Lilbourne

The Devil's Den at Fyfield Hill, near Marlborough

Sunset walk around Stonehenge (Photographed from the permissive path)

Scratchbury Camp Iron Age hill fort

Autumn colours at Battlesbury Iron Age hill fort, near Warminster

Cley Hill Iron Age hill fort near Warminster

Tinhead Hill Neolithic long barrow, under the fan tree on Salisbury Plain

WILTSHIRE WHITE HORSES

Alton Barnes White Horse

White Horse in the village of Broad Town

Cherhill White Horse and Lansdowne monument

Devizes White Horse, seen from the Devizes green

Hackpen White Horse near the village of Broad Hinton

Pewsey White Horse

Westbury White Horse

TOWNS AND CITY OF SALISBURY

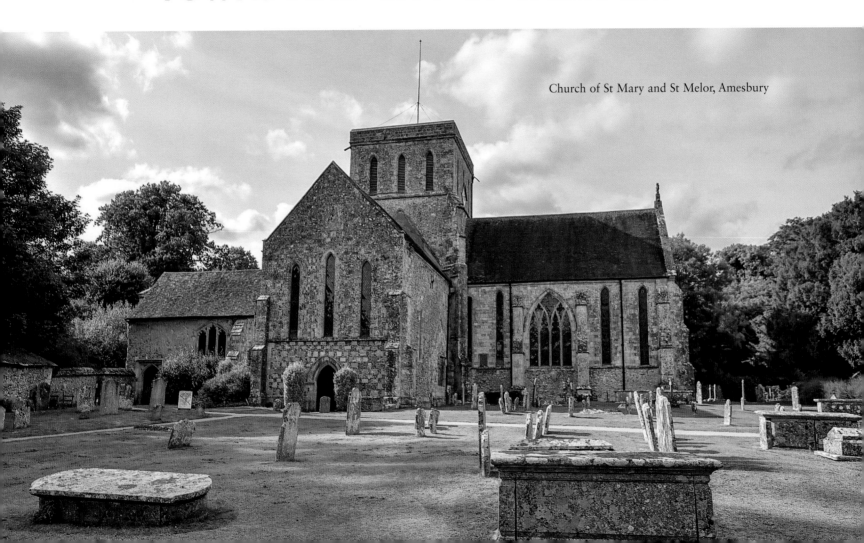

Church of St Mary and St Melor, Amesbury

Bradford-on-Avon town bridge

The riverside in Bradford-on-Avon during spring

Looking towards St Mary's Church, Calne

Beech Terrace, Calne

The Buttercross, Chippenham

Springtime in John Coles Park, Chippenham

Corsham Town Hall

Row of cottages in Cricklade high street

The fountain, marketplace, Devizes

Devizes marketplace and market cross

Highworth high street

The twelfth-century Ludgershall Castle

Snowdrops grow in the grounds of Malmesbury Abbey

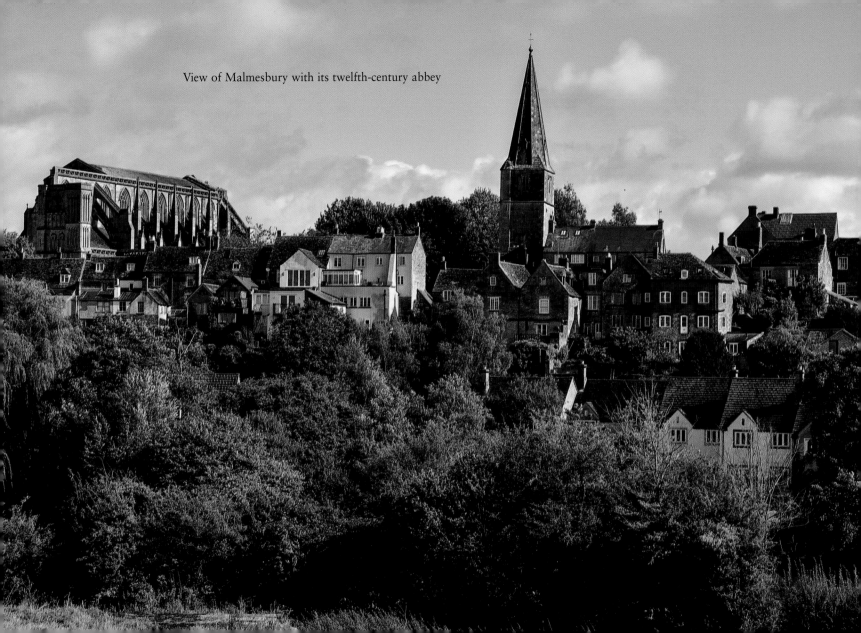

View of Malmesbury with its twelfth-century abbey

Marlborough Town Hall

Melksham Town Hall

View over the town
from Castle Hill, Mere

Royal Wootton Bassett Town Hall

Salisbury Cathedral in the springtime

Salisbury town gate

Swindon railway village

Bandstand in Swindon
town gardens

Tedworth House, Tidworth, the home of Help for Heroes

Trowbridge war memorial in the town park

Warminster Grade II obelisk, built in 1783

Westbury war memorial and cottages

St Mary's Church
ruins, Wilton

VILLAGES

Biddestone village green

Bluebells in bloom, Castle Combe

Castle Combe under blue skies

Spring arrives in the village of Easterton

Golden light shines upon Edington Priory Church

Village of Erlestoke in springtime

Marston 2
Worton 3

LOWER ROAD

Great Cheverell high street

Horse riders enjoy
a ride through
Heytesbury

Green leafy trees line the road into Hindon

Geese on the river
at Horningsham

Kington St Michael

A touch of autumn colour in Lacock

King Alfred statue, Pewsey, unveiled in 1913

Sherrington Pond and cottages

Sherston high street

Steeple Ashton lock-up and market cross

Tisbury village centre

Ducks gather at Urchfont Pond

The bell inn and St Mary's Church, Wylye

Peacock outside Yatton Keynell Church

WILTSHIRE LANDSCAPES

Luccombe Bottom, Bratton

Daffodils in the spring sunshine at Bowood Gardens

Crop circle in a farmer's field near Bratton

The lush green landscape of the Deverills

Path through the yellow rapeseed field at Dilton Marsh

Harvest time in the village of Edington

Fonthill Archway on the Fonthill estate

Vibrant countryside at Market Lavington

Regimental badges cut into the chalk hillside at Fovant

Longleat House viewed from Heaven's Gate, Warminster

Sunshine on Lydiard House after a rainstorm

Marden harvest stooks drying in the sunshine

Maud Heath's Causeway

Middle Hill, Warminster

Farming in the Pewsey Vale

Signs at the start of the Ridgeway at Overton Hill

The Ridgeway, an ancient trackway and Britain's oldest road

Lush landscape seen from the Ridgeway

Rolling countryside, the Wessex Downs

Countryside near the village of Broad Hinton

Roundway Hill in the autumn sunshine

Red campion flower meadow on the Salisbury Plain

Field of yellow rapeseed on the Salisbury Plain

St Mary's Church, Steeple Ashton

Farmer bringing in the harvest in the Wiltshire countryside

Paragliders soar over the landscape from the Westbury White Horse

Wilton Windmill in the golden hour sunshine

View from the top of Win Green over
Cranborne Chase

Looking towards Woodborough Hill in the Pewsey Vale

Stone sculptures at Heaven's Gate, Warminster

Highworth wind turbines on a summer's day

Snow covers the Wiltshire landscape

WATER AND WOODLANDS

Sunrise at Shearwater Lake, Crockerton

Swan on the River Avon from Bulford Bridge

Boats moored at Pewsey Wharf

Canal boats on the Kennet and Avon Canal near Pewsey

Narrowboat passes through a lock at Semington

Chaveywell Bridge, Castlefields
Canal and River Park, Calne

Westbury fishing lake overlooked by the White Horse

Flock of Canadian geese on the water at Caenhill, Devizes

Autumn has arrived at the Caenhill Locks, Devizes

Crammer Pond, Devizes

Fonthill Lake on the Fonthill estate

The hamlet of Reybridge, near Lacock

Warminster Town Park in the autumn

Autumnal golden light at Langford Lakes

Wilts & Berks Canal at Chippenham

Bluebell Woods, West Woods, near Marlborough

Woodland walk at Bowood

Wild garlic woodland above the village of Castle Combe

Bluebells in bloom in Erlestoke Wood

Rhododendrons by Heaven's Gate, Warminster

Avenue of trees at Clanger Wood, near Westbury

Autumn in the woodland at Clanger Wood, near Westbury

Autumn colours at Biss Wood, Trowbridge

The avenue of golden trees at Savernake Forest, Marlborough